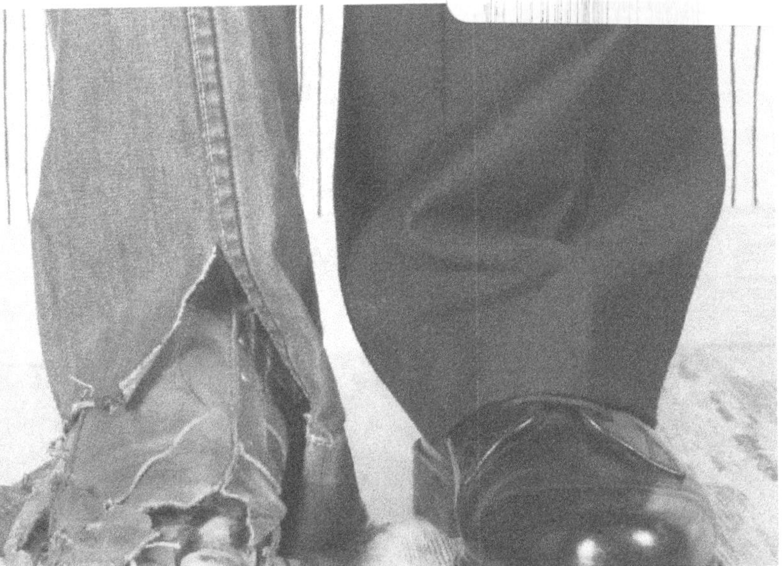

SEVEN DIFFERENCES BETWEEN THE RICH AND THE POOR

WHY THE RICH ARE RICH AND THE POOR POOR

Feyi Abraham Adesanya

SEVEN DIFFERENCES BETWEEN THE RICH AND THE POOR
(Why the Rich are Rich and the Poor Poor)

Copyright © 2018
Feyi Abraham Adesanya

First Print: August 2018

All rights reserved. No portion may be reproduced, stored in a retrieval system or transmitted in any form or by any means - electronic, mechanical, photocopying, recording, scanning or other except for the brief Quotation in critical reviews or articles without the prior written permission of the author.

All Bible Quotations are from the Authorized King James Version.

Cover Design, Page Layout & Print
Cypresshill Concepts: 0802 422 8141, 0803 798 6872

DEDICATION

Much like we recognize that the scriptures
were written by God even though men penned
down the words, this book was only penned by
me, the actual author is God himself and to
Him therefore this book is dedicated.

ACKNOWLEGEMENT

My appreciation goes to all friends and
partners of THE TEACHER MINISTRIES
all over the world. Your love and support for this
work of the ministry is one thing God has used
to sustain us thus far. I pray God continues to
reward your efforts and labour, may you be
empowered to do more for the kingdom of God.

CONTENTS

Introduction

Chapter 1	7
(Lucky to be Rich, Destined to be Poor)	
Chapter 2	12
(Three Ms Of Money)	
Chapter 3	17
(Reward vs Gift)	
Chapter 4	21
(Reality vs Mentality)	
Chapter 5	26
(Priority)	
Chapter 6	30
(Focus)	
Chapter 7	36
(Penny Wise, Pounds Foolish)	

INTRODUCTION

If there is a redistribution of all of the world's wealth such that everybody gets the same amount of money, we will find out that in just a matter of time, some people will become poor and others become rich, almost all (if not all) of those who were poor before the redistribution will be poor again and almost all (if not all) of those who were rich before the redistribution will be rich again. This is because having money does not necessarily make you rich, likewise, your lack of money does not necessarily mean that you are poor. There are attitudes towards money that attract money and there are attitudes towards money that repel it. These things are the actual things that make the rich rich and the poor poor.

Highlighted in this book are some seven different attitudes that differentiates the rich from the poor. Going through them, you will find where you belong and how you can switch, what mindset you are holding on to that is responsible for your present financial state and whether you are heading towards poverty or prosperity. These same things differentiate not just rich persons from the poor but also rich countries and organizations from the poor.

Chapter 1

Lucky to be Rich, Destined to be Poor.

Many poor people see the rich as just being fortunate and themselves unfortunate whereas, the rich is rich because of certain principles he is applying. Yes, it is true that we don't get the same opportunities to be rich in life (we actually don't need to) but we all will get our own fair share of opportunities to be rich. To attribute riches to luck is to say that it doesn't matter what you do or don't do, it is all a matter of luck, and nothing can be farther from the truth than that. Of course, there is the grace factor (which by the way is available to all) but that does not replace responsibility on our part.

1 Corinthians 15:10 says

"But by the grace of God I am what I am: and his grace which was bestowed upon me was not in vain; but I labored more abundantly than they all: yet not I but the grace of God which was with me."

Paul attributed his success to the grace factor and rightly so but he didn't fail to tell us that he also laboured. In fact, he said if he didn't labour the grace of God would have been in vain over him.

Lucky To Be Rich, Destined To Be Poor

It is dangerous to believe in luck, those who do are hardly lucky. Someone said "success is a function of luck, ask any failure". The moment you attribute riches or even success in general to luck, you give up your ability to determine your fate, you are now completely at the mercy of "merciless" luck.

If you are presently poor (that is, you don't have money) be willing to learn what you can do differently to better your lot, don't explain it away on luck, don't lock yourself in. If you are rich, please don't also attribute it to luck, it is dangerous to succeed without knowing how, should anything go wrong, you won't know how to reproduce the wealth. That's the irony of luck, it favours nobody, at least not for long.

This concept of luck is what keeps many people betting and gambling away their fortune hoping that one day "Mr.Lucky" will smile on them but alas he hardly smiles and even when he does, he soon frowns at the same person he smiled at. Those who make money luckily soon run out of luck, that's why you discover that most people who win or inherit huge sums of money end up poor one way or the other, why?

You may make money by luck but you certainly cannot manage it by luck. So, if you see someone who has been able to maintain riches for a considerable length of time, it is certainly not luck, he knows a thing or two about money that is keeping him or her going.

Closely related to luck but more dangerous is the belief that whoever is rich is rich because God destined him or her to be rich. I say this is more dangerous because it is religious in nature. If that is true, it would mean that we'll just have to accept (or should I say suffer) whatever fate befalls us since God cannot be questioned. Those who have this mindset erroneously base it on scriptures like:

Deuteronomy 15:11
"For the poor shall never cease out of the land…"

John 12:8
"For the poor always ye have with you; but me ye have not always"

They interpret this to mean that God makes some poor, that's why He (God) said there will always be poor people.

Unfortunately, that's not what those portions of scripture mean. Yes, there will always be poor people in the land, that's because there will always be (sadly so) people who have wrong attitude towards money and consequently make wrong decisions about money. God does not destine anybody to be poor. It is actually your choice to be among the rich in the land or among the poor. It is neither luck nor fate.

Chapter 2

Three Ms of Money

There are three Ms of money, namely; **Make**, **Manage** and **Multiply**. Of course, the rich know how to make money but the poor also know how to make money (at least to some degree), what differentiates them significantly are the other two Ms of money; how to manage and how to multiply money. How many times have we seen people who made huge amounts of money during the peak of their career and business only to declare bankruptcy a few years after and then there are some who didn't make extra-ordinary amount of money at a go but through good management end up wealthy? I like the way Proverbs 13:11 puts it **"Wealth GOTTEN by vanity shall be diminished: but he that GATHERETH by labour shall increase"**

There are those who just get (or make) money and there are those who go beyond getting to gathering, that talks of management and multiplication. The former are the poor, because they know next to nothing about managing and multiplying money, they concentrate so much on making money that if for some reasons can't make as much money as they want, they turn to crime.

They may have at the moment a well-paying job or a thriving business and are making good money but as they are making the money, there is no plan for savings, investments and such like things. For them financial literacy and intelligence is overrated. They don't know the difference between an asset and a liability, their expenses are almost at par with their income (sometimes it is even above). Their life is good until either they lose their job or their business collapses or there is a recession or they retire. Unfortunately, they are used to a particular lifestyle but now that lifestyle can no longer be maintained since money isn't coming in the way it used to come in before and there are no backups.

Truly they brought in some hunt, but they were too lazy to process what they hunted as Proverbs 12:27 aptly describes them:

"The slothful man roasteth not that which he took in hunting: but the substance of a diligent man is precious"

A hunter who doesn't roast what he caught in hunting will:

1. Waste the hunt because an unroasted hunt will soon spoil.
2. The hunter will have to go a hunting every day otherwise he will die of hunger.

Whereas if he had roasted yesterday's hunt, there would have been enough left for a few more days. That's what happens to people who make good money but are actually poor minded, they waste the money and end up in need.

The sad thing about these people is that they are very gifted people and so making money kind of comes easy to them and they sit on that at the expense of money management and multiplication. The rich on the other hand are more disciplined when it comes to money management, they prioritize things like savings and investments. They are always looking for how to multiply their income and income streams while reducing their expenses. They work for money just like every other person but unlike the poor, they make their money also work for them. They are like Joseph, they read the seasons, they know when it is "seven years of plenty" and what to do with it in order to survive the coming "seven years of famine". When they retire, lose their jobs, or business goes down or there is a recession, they are not shaken. In fact, they wax stronger.

As it is with individuals, so also it is with organizations and nations. The poorest nations are usually the most gifted and they make good enough money too, it is poor management that makes them poor. On the other hand, it is good management that makes rich nations rich, most of them are not anywhere as gifted as their poor counterparts.

So, if you want to be rich (which I believe you want to otherwise you wouldn't be reading this book), don't just "make" money, go for knowledge on how to manage and multiply money, be financially literate so you can be money wise.

CHAPTER 3

REWARD VS GIFT

"You have money; therefore, you should give me some" is the reasoning of the poor, the rich thinks thus: what can I do for you in exchange for your money? The former thinks of money primarily as a gift, the latter sees it as a reward. No doubt, giving should be encouraged, after all the bible says in Ephesians 4:28 that: "Let him that stole steal no more: but rather let him labour with his hands the thing which is good, **THAT HE MAY HAVE TO GIVE TO HIM THAT NEEDETH**"

That does not and should not mean that the needy should remain on welfare forever. God expects the poor to strive to be rich too.

Nobody becomes rich on welfare, handouts and hand downs. Nobody who has a sense of entitlement gets rich either. It is poverty mindedness that makes people get angry at rich people who are not giving them their money, nobody owes anybody anything! Have you ever seen a beggar given (let's say) a billion Nigerian naira? No, it doesn't happen. You know why? Money is primarily a reward for value given not a gift that's why even when people give money, they give in accordance to value such that they tend to give more to the man who already has (who is valuable to them) than the man who doesn't have (who is not valuable to them). So, you'll find a millionaire gift his millionaire friend millions of naira on his birthday but manage to drop a five hundred naira bill for the beggar on the street. The beggar obviously needs the money more but money flows in the direction of value. It will be way easier to get a million naira from someone for whom you have done something worth a million naira than begging the same person for a million naira. Money is a means of exchange, everybody is willing to exchange it for something they want or need, you offer them what they want and their pockets open to you. That my friend is the paradigm of the rich.

Remember the prodigal son in Luke chapter 15? He said to his father "give me"- verse 12. All of a sudden he had money but he wasn't rich, he soon realized it. You see, 'give me' is the language of the poor; poor people and poor nations alike. Many third world leaders keep asking for one aid or the other but alas they are not bettered by it. Don't get me wrong, there is nothing wrong in asking for help when you really need it but to be satisfied living off the benevolence of another person is unhealthy and unhelpful to you. When life taught the prodigal son a tough lesson on money, his approach and indeed his language changed. Hitherto he said "give me" but now he said "make me…"- Luke 15:19. Hear him: *"And am no more worthy to be called thy son: make me as one of thy hired servants"*

Before, he just wanted to inherit money, now he wants to earn it. On hearing this, the father was so elated that he threw him a party.

When you begin to think like this reformed prodigal son, you are on your way to wealth. You will begin to think in terms of goods and services to offer to people in exchange for their money instead of begging them for it. When you beg, they give you peanut if at all they give you and you are forced to say thank you but if you trade with them, they pay you what the trade is worth and still thank you for solving their problems. I don't know about you but I think I like the latter.

Chapter 4

Reality vs Mentality

Seven Differences Between The Rich And The Poor

The story is told of a rich man who went bankrupt but on passing by a poor beggar gave the beggar the last cash on him. When asked why he did that considering his present financial state, he replied "the beggar is poor, I am only broke". There is a difference between being rich and having money, you can have money and really not be rich, likewise you can be rich but at the moment broke. Upon giving the beggar that money, the beggar suddenly had more money than the broke man but he lacks the correct knowledge and mentality about money that can make him rich, the broke man on the other hand is armed with the right knowledge and mentality about money that can make him bounce back in no time. Added to that is the fact that he has rich friends from whom he can get some support. So, their reality may be the same, but their mentality is not at all and that is what makes the difference.

For the poor, being rich is all about having money but for the rich it is first of all a mentality before a reality. There are actually mentalities that attract money to you, likewise, there are mentalities that repel money from you.

For example, the thinking that there is no money in a particular place is a faulty and poor mentality, there is money everywhere there are people and even if the people in your location are not rich, you can always attract money from outside that location into it because money follows value. Another mentality difference is their interpretation of things; where a rich man sees a business opportunity, a poor man sees problems, yet they are looking at the same thing.

Riches has a lot to do with what and how you think; you think poor, you become poor, you think rich, you grow rich. The scriptures put it this way:

Proverbs 23:7
"…as he thinketh in his heart, so is he…"
Mentality is more powerful than reality, your mentality will over time override your reality, that is why a man who has money today but thinks like a poor man will soon become poor and a man who doesn't have money today but thinks like a rich man will sooner or later become rich. It's not so hard to know someone with a poor mentality, all you need do is listen to them talk about money, after all as the scripture says "out of the abundance of the heart, the mouth speaketh"- Matthew 12:34. Statements like "where will I

get that kind of money from?", "only a thief can have that amount of money", "there is no money anywhere", "those rich people" are indicative of a mentality skewed towards poverty. If you catch yourself saying things like these, its time you obey Romans 12:2- renew your mind! On the other hand, the rich mentality talks like this "I may not have that kind of money yet, but I will work towards it" "There is money in this land, I will get my portion".

The poor man's mentality works like those small calculators that display an error message the moment you are trying to do big figures. When he hears one million naira (for instance) and he doesn't have it, his brain immediately shuts down. His rich counterpart on the other hand (who may at the moment also not have the money) thinks like this- "one million naira is just one thousand naira in one thousand places, or ten thousand in hundred places, or hundred thousand in ten places… If I can get five people who can give me two hundred thousand each or do ten turn overs of a hundred-thousand-naira profit business I can make a million naira". The rich mentality unlike the poor isn't harassed by big amount of money, it demystifies it by breaking it down and chewing it in pieces.

I notice also that the poor mentality doesn't know the difference between expensiveness and affordability, the poor man uses these two words interchangeably. To him, "It is expensive" is the same with "I can't afford it" but no it isn't and the rich knows this. Many times, you will find the poor man explain away very important things just because he can't afford it. Tell him of a good school for his children, the moment you mention the fees, you will hear something like "is it not just to teach books?" he thinks it is expensive but the problem is actually that he can't afford it. Something is expensive only if the cost outweighs its benefits. When you can't afford something yet, say so and be sure to put "yet" which means that you are not ruling out the possibility of being able to afford it tomorrow but don't say something is expensive just because you can't afford it yet otherwise you will be repelling money unknowingly.

CHAPTER 5

PRIORITY

Money is very revealing; there is no denying, what you spend your money on the most is what is most important to you. Where your money goes, your life goes. Your spending priority not only speak volume of who you are and who you are becoming but it is also creating for you a financial future. Hear what the bible says: **Proverbs 21:17**

"He that loveth pleasure shall be a poor man: he that loveth wine and oil shall not be rich"

Now, is God against pleasure or wine and oil (which are symbolic of luxury)? Certainly not. What the scripture is saying is that if pleasure and luxury is your topmost priority in life, you will undoubtedly become poor. If we consider the fact that that particular scripture was penned down by the rich king Solomon, you'll know that it must be true. When we look at the expenditure of the poor man vis a vis his income, we'll discover that he spends first and most on pleasure. You will find that very little or in fact nothing of his income is spent on the important things of life; a book of #1,000 is expensive but not a bottle of #10,000 bottle of wine, earning is more important to him than learning, he prioritizes getting the latest gadgets over paying for a seminar that can change his life. The funny thing is that if he continues like that, sooner or later he won't be able to afford the pleasure he so much loves. The rich too like pleasure and luxury (who doesn't?), it's just that they understand that certain things are more important hence they spend last and least on it.

Ironically poor people love pleasure more than the rich (or so it seems), haven't you seen people struggle financially to use gadgets, clothings and accessories that many rich people don't bother about? I think it gives them a false sense of identity and that's a problem on its own because as the scripture says,

"…a man's life consisteth not in the abundance of the things which he possesseth."- **Luke 12:15**

The love for luxury and pleasure will not only leak away your money, it will also reduce your earning ability, in other words it destroys you financially from both the expenditure column and the income column. Laziness often accompanies the love for pleasure, more often than not, lovers of luxury can't work hard enough to conveniently live the life they dream of so they continue to live in a bubble until of course the bubble bursts. The rich works hard and therefore earns enough for him to enjoy the luxuries of life conveniently and not at the expense of more important things of life.

Priority

By the time you are having to loan money for pleasure and luxury, you are driving towards poverty. In more developed climes, people easily make this mistake because of the easy accessibility of credits. So, they find themselves spending what they haven't earned and the advertising industry does a good job in ensuring most of that money ends up on luxuries; things they can very well do without or at least postpone till a time they can conveniently afford it but no, their love for luxury keeps driving them further and further into poverty.

Chapter 6

Focus

Seven Differences Between The Rich And The Poor

Focus is yet another thing that differentiates the rich from the poor and makes some people rich and others poor. Everybody has one thing or the other, there is nobody who doesn't have anything at all, God ensures this. Also, nobody has everything, no matter how rich you are, there will be certain things you still don't have. So, at every point in time, there will be things you have and things you don't have. What makes the rich rich is that they focus on what they have and use it maximally. As they do, they get more and more of what they don't have but need, in other words, they use what they have to get what they don't have. The poor on the other hand is so fixated on what he doesn't have that he fails to realize the value and power of what he actually has till eventually he loses even what he has.

Luke 19:26

"For I say unto you, that unto everyone which hath shall be given and from him that hath not, even that he hath shall be taken away from him"

This is why the rich keep getting richer and the poor poorer. It is not the unfairness of life, it is a principle of life has established by God that if you use well whatever you have, you will have more and if you don't use well or worse still don't use at all what you have (because you think it is small or nothing), you will lose it and guess who will gain it- the one who used his well. This is well illustrated by Jesus' parable of talents- Matthew 25:14-29. The man who was given one talent who failed to use it eventually lost it to the man who turned his five talent into ten.

Matthew 25:26-28
"His lord answered and said unto him, Thou wicked and slothful servant, thou knewest that I reap where I sowed not, and gather where I have not strawed:

Thou oughtest therefore to have put my money to the exchangers, and then at my coming I should have received mine own with usury.

Take therefore the talent from him, and give it unto him which hath ten talents."

Focus

What makes the poor poor is not because he was given just one talent while others were given more to start, what makes him poor is his failure to trade his talent. Steve Harris puts it this way – "it's not what you don't have that limits you, it's what you have but don't know how to use"

The poor man is always thinking and saying "If only I have this or that", his attention is almost always on what he doesn't have at the expense of what he does have. He hardly ever says "this is what I have, what can I do with it?". If he were Peter at the temple's beautiful gate (Acts chapter three), he would have just told the lame man "Silver and Gold have I none" he wouldn't have added "such as I have, give I thee". You may at the moment not have money, but look well, there are things you have that can be used in place of money or even traded for money. It may be time, ideas, knowledge, skill, experience or relationships. That's your money! You see, money is just a medium of exchange, you can't eat it, you can't bath with it, you can't even play with it, you just can't do anything with it other than trade it for something else you want.

Everyone who has it therefore is willing to trade it for the other things they need. What that means is that if you can offer them what they want and how they want it, you can have some of their money but as long as you keep focusing on what you don't have, you still won't have and in fact what you have will begin to diminish. The law of focus states that "what you focus on increases". Master what you have, develop it and trade it- that's how you become rich.

In 2nd Kings chapter four, verse one through seven, we are told of the story of a poor widow at the brink of bankruptcy, her two sons were about to be taken because of the debt she and her late husband owed. She ran to Prophet Elijah for help and the man of God asked her two questions, the first being "what can I do for you?"- verse 2. For some reasons we don't know, she didn't answer this question, I want to believe she figured out that the answer holds no permanent solution to her financial problems. At best, Elijah would clear her debts and possibly give her a little stipend that will sooner or later finish and she will be back in need. That first question is good enough for the poor though, but the rich will go for Elijah's second question as did the widow -"what do you have in your house?"

After careful thought, she realized she had a bottle of oil and that was enough to turn around her fortune. God multiplied it and she started a business out of it that sustained her throughout her lifetime.

If you can answer two questions well, you will sooner or later be rich. What are these questions? "what do I have?" and "what can I do with it?"

Chapter 7

Penny Wise, Pounds Foolish

Seven Differences Between The Rich And The Poor

I first heard this statement from my mother, I knew it long before I understood it. A person who is penny wise but pounds foolish is smart (or seemingly so) when it comes to small monies but foolish when it comes to huge amount of money. They make money in pennies but lose money in pounds in the long haul. Their micro-economics looks great but their macro-economics very poor, they are short-sighted in their financial decisions and dealings, they think only of the present and so make financial decisions that jeopardize their future, consequently they become poor. He is ready to gain a few extra bucks from a client at the expense of retainership. They cannot delay gratification, in fact they won't do anything that won't pay "now now" as we say in our local parlance.

There is a private university in a neighbouring country of ours here in west Africa that wanted to buy land from a community in order to build, they proposed to the heads of the community that they would pay about half of the valued price but will allow the community have on a yearly basis five students on full scholarship in the school. Guess what, the community turned down the offer, they wanted the full amount and the full amount they got. Its been well over a decade now, the money is of course spent but they can't afford to send their wards to the very school they host. Now that's a classic example of penny wise pounds foolish, a case of Esau and Jacob. The poor often don't see the big picture, somethings may cost you a little now but will save you a whole lot in the long haul but they don't know

It is actually cheaper to be rich, the poor eventually pays more for almost everything. For instance, while 75ml of a grocery item goes for (let's say) 500 Nigerian Naira, the 150ml pack of the same grocery usually goes for about #900 instead of #1000. The poor man buys the 75ml pack and then it finishes, goes back to buy another by which time he has spent #100 extra than his rich counterpart who buys the 150ml pack and that is just on one item. If you calculate that over everything he buys over a long period of time, you will be shocked the amount of money he is losing unknowingly. Now, I understand that sometimes he is constrained by cash hence he can't buy the "#150ml pack" but I do know also that sometimes, there are friends, colleagues and neighbours of his in the same shoes with whom he can join funds, get it and share while working towards being able to single handedly afford it. That mentality of "how to get the best bargain possible" is one major reason the rich are rich, they are constantly weighing their options and considering better alternatives.

When you opt to buy an obviously inferior product because it is cheaper than the original not because you don't have the money but because you think the original is expensive, you will end up paying more when of course the inferior product spoils and you keep repairing or you have to buy another one or the inferior product spoils something else because it is inferior, you are penny wise. Learn to see the big picture and not just the seeming immediate gain. Learn to see the cumulative effect of your financial dealings and act appropriately.

POSTSCRIPT

CHOOSING TO FOLLOW JESUS

It will be robbery to have shared with you in this book all that I have shared and not give you an opportunity to accept Jesus into your life.

Jesus died to save us all from our sins and from everlasting damnation; He came to make us children of God. Anyone who dies without receiving Jesus is damned forever; you must not let that happen to you. I challenge you today, if you have not done it before, to accept to follow and live for Jesus from today.

If you want to accept Him into your life, from your heart say this simple prayer:

"Jesus, I acknowledge that I am a sinner and helpless without you. Today, I accept you as my saviour from sin. Forgive me of every sin I have ever committed and please cleanse me from every form of defilement. Come and take your place in my life and make me yours. Thank you for hearing me. Amen"

It may even be that you just need to rededicate your life to Him; If that is the case, just ask Him to forgive you and take you back. You may say the prayer above as a re-affirmation of your faith.

Find a bible-believing church within your neighbourhood and begin to fellowship with them, they will explain the way of the Lord more to you and help you grow in your new-found faith. God bless You!

NOTES

LETS'S CONNECT

Facebook : Feyi Abraham Adesanya,
              The Teacher Ministries
Twitter: @FeyiAdesanya
Instagram:@feyi_abraham_adesanya
YouTube: The Teacher Ministries
e-mail: feyiabrahamadesanya@gmail.com
              theteacherministries@gmail.com
Blog: www.theteacherministries.wordpress.com

www.ingramcontent.com/pod-product-compliance
Lightning Source LLC
Chambersburg PA
CBHW070139230526
45472CB00004B/1603